Worship and Mission

Worship and Mission

Dave Bilbrough

New Wine Press

New Wine Ministries
PO Box 17
Chichester
West Sussex
United Kingdom
PO19 2AW

Copyright © 2006 Dave Bilbrough

All rights reserved. No part of this publication may be reproduced, stored in a retrieval system, or transmitted in any form or by any means, electronic, mechanical, photocopying or otherwise, without the prior written consent of the publisher. Short extracts may be used for review purposes.

Unless indicated otherwise, Scripture quotations are taken from The Holy Bible, New International Version. Copyright © 1973, 1978, 1984 by International Bible Society. Used by permission of Hodder and Stoughton Limited.

NKJV – The Holy Bible, New King James Version. Copyright © 1982 by Thomas Nelson Inc.

The Message by Eugene H. Peterson, copyright © 1993, 1994, 1995, 2000, 2001, 2002. Used by permission of NavPress Publishing Group. All rights reserved.

NLT – New Living Translation. Copyright © 1996, 2004 by Tyndale Charitable Trust. Used by permission of Tyndale House Publishers.

ISBN-10: 1-903725-76-3
ISBN-13: 978-1-903725-76-4

Typeset by CRB Associates, Reepham, Norfolk
Cover design by CCD, www.ccdgroup.co.uk
Printed in Malta

Acknowledgements

Along with all the usual suspects mentioned in my last book, including Adrian and Pauline Hawkes and my wonderful band, I would very much like to thank Norman and Grace Barnes, Rich Hubbard, John and Christine Noble, Les Moir, Martin Neil, Jenny Sinnadurai and Karen Dcy – each of whom has inspired me along with others to expand the journey.

Thanks also to Clive Price and Adam Harbinson who provoked me to write on these themes.

To Rainbow church, as well as my many friends around the world, who are out there doing it and are such an inspiration to me .

Tim Pettingale, for once again believing in this project.

Jan Doidge, my tremendously hardworking secretary.

To Dan (Secret), Jon and Ros, and my ever-loving wife, Pat.

Foreword

This book is invaluable to those who want their lives to make a difference in this world. It will give faith that our music can unite people, disarm people and show the beauty of a Living God to people. Dave is the real deal and his life of worship has been a mission we have all watched and respected. Let his years of insight show us how to open up the doors and let the music play.

Martin Smith (Delirious?)

Worship for sale (or sail!)

> I'm sailing on a sea of love
> And the wind is blowing free
> I have put my faith in a simple trust that my God
>   will be with me
> Yes I've nailed my colours to the mast
> Set my course, I'm on the move
> There'll be many dangers up ahead
> But my God will see me through.[1]

This song that I wrote a while back represents significant developments in my own focus and calling that have accelerated over time. Being old enough to remember a time before off-white Hallelujah song sheets, OHPs and electro-acoustic guitars, my life has long been immersed in worship and the creation of meaningful expressions.

Now, as many across the globe are experiencing and enjoying the phenomenal growth of contemporary worship music with its unprecedented popularity reaching into every part of church culture and infrastructure, the compass hand I am learning to follow has gradually been leading me on a path to

[1] Dave Bilbrough © 1997 Thankyou Music. Taken from the album *Secret Places*.

make this spirit of worship known and accessible to our fractured yet beautiful world.

> "In an era where the popularity of contemporary worship music around the world is unsurpassed, where CDs, songbooks and conferences abound, it is easy to forget the relationship between our music and our mission."

A.W. Tozer influenced many, including myself, with his inspiring book *Worship – the Missing Jewel of the Evangelical Church*.[2] It proved to be a provocative and insightful encouragement to reclaim much territory that had been lost in our worship. A friend, however, recently quipped to me that Tozer writing to this current generation would probably have to rephrase his title to read: "Worship and its Commercialisation in the Modern Day Church". An interesting statement but perhaps, sadly, at times one that is not too far from the truth. In an era where the popularity of contemporary worship music around the world is unsurpassed, where CDs, songbooks and conferences abound, it is easy to forget the relationship between our music and our mission.

Recently I heard a TV evangelist quoting the startling statistic that 96% of preaching is directed

[2] A.W. Tozer, *Worship – the Missing Jewel of the Evangelical Church*, Christian Publications, 1996.

towards 6% of the world's population. To quote Oswald Chambers, "Many of us talk of the Second Coming when half the world has not heard of the first." Untold millions are still untold and God's heart beats with compassion for the lost.

Apparently the average church-going Westerner has listened to 8,000 sermons and joined in 15,000 prayers, and after all that very few have led another to faith in Christ. As Chambers stated: "Our worship must be linked with mission." This sentiment sums up our relationship with the world and how we need to see mission.

Just as Nero practised his fiddle while Rome was burning we need to ensure that we do not allow ourselves to become distracted from seeing a world in desperate need of the Saviour. As my friends from the popular Christian band *Delirious?* would put it: it's time for us to let that mission bell ring loud and clear.

Recently I was invited to be interviewed by a radio station. As a songwriter/worship leader this is not an unusual occurrence for me and I enjoy the opportunity of sharing my faith, and often my life story, with the wider audience that this presents. This particular interview offered me a challenge, however. Scheduled to take place in the north of England, I already had a prior commitment in the London area some hours away that would prevent me from realistically doing the journey in time and attending in person. A compromise was reached and a local radio station in London was

Worship and Mission

enlisted for me to do a live link up with the northern station, giving the impression to the listener that I was actually present in the studio in the north.

I arrived in good time in London, entered a small, cramped studio, sparsely furnished with just a table, chair and a microphone, and engaged happily with the interviewer, who was in the north, in a two-way conversation prior to going live. Just a few minutes before the interview took place we hit a major problem. I could be heard live on-air, but the interviewer, the one asking me the questions, would not be able to be heard. Soon we would be going to the news and weather and the theme tune for the programme would start. A hasty conversation took place over my mobile with the apologetic interviewer. "Time is so short... don't know what to do," he said breathlessly. "All I can suggest right now is that you interview yourself!" The coming news and subsequent beckoning theme tune rather forced my hand in a hasty affirmative response. "What else can I do?" I thought.

For the next hour I subsequently interviewed myself. It's amazing how I did it when I think about it, but somehow, with one eye on the clock I managed to fulfil my one-hour commitment. Relieved, yet somehow triumphant I strolled down the road outside. "How did I manage to get through that?" I wondered. Yet, as I played the events back in my mind, I must admit I kept returning to this dominant thought: "I may have got through it, but did I really answer any of the questions that people really wanted to know? Was this conversation with myself just a mere opportunity to think aloud or did it help or genuinely synchronise with the needs of others?" There I was in this confined environment talking to myself, unaware of the wider picture in the world outside. In the same way has our preoccupation with worship become an opportunity for us to escape and close our eyes to the genuine needs that are around us? I want a worship that is real, spiritual and yet tangible, revealing the presence of God in the material, fusing heaven with earth like the bread and wine of communion, satisfying not only the spiritual craving but the hunger pangs and cries for freedom that I am surrounded by and that are flashed on my TV screen on a daily basis.

> **"Worship without mission is self-indulgent; mission without worship is self-defeating."**
> Graham Cray

The altar and the tent

(Read Genesis 12:7–8; 13:3–4, 18)

Throughout his life, Abraham (formerly known as Abram) was continually building altars as acts of

Worship and Mission

worship to the God who had appeared to him. In Genesis 12 we see how, as a result of the altar being built, the tent comes into view. Abraham pitched his tent in various places and worshipped God wherever he went. The altar represents our response of worship to God; the tent represents our moving out into the world. In chapters 12 and 13 we see the two become inseparable. Wherever there is an altar (a true act of worship) there will be a response that eventually leads to us actively engaging with the world around us.

In true worship God speaks to us. We answer by responding in a way that will fulfil His purposes out in the world. The stories of the callings of Jeremiah and Isaiah tell us how divine interaction took place with these individuals to produce not only a personal response, but also a response that would have consequences to others.

I witnessed a contemporary example of this when I had the pleasure of meeting Derek and Gill Atkins on a recent trip to Uganda. They headed up a remarkable work in conjunction with Mildmay Hospital[3] serving the many sufferers of AIDS in that region of Africa. As I walked around the grounds I was so impressed by their commitment, their professionalism that was of the highest standard, coupled with their evident compassion for the victims of this deadly and incurable disease. Later as we talked in their office

---

[3] Mildmay is a Christian organisation dedicated to improving the lives of men, women and children challenged by HIV and AIDS.

Worship and Mission

I was intrigued to hear their story – how they came from the suburban county of Kent to be there – and I discovered that it was at Spring Harvest just a few years ago, Europe's largest Bible teaching and worship event, that they felt a clear call to embrace this adventure of faith that they were now journeying on. Like so many, it was there in the environment of worship that God had clearly commissioned them. Out of worship God speaks and His heart is always for mission. A true act of worship is when we respond and use our gifts in practical ways for His glory – a worship of Jesus who came not to be served, but to serve.

> **"Our calling is to be just like Abraham, to be blessed, but not to stop there. We must then be a blessing to others. Worship and mission are inseparably linked."**

At the start of each day I enjoy a good shower to freshen me for work. It's great, but I can't live in the shower! The shower is to prepare me for the events of the day in the same way the showers of blessing that God wants to pour out on us are designed to make us active participants, not just passive observers in this world. Our calling is to be just like Abraham, to be

Worship and Mission

blessed, but not to stop there. We must then be a blessing to others. Worship and mission are inseparably linked.

The altars that Abraham built would have been for burnt sacrifices. This is very distinct from the sin offering or blood offering. Depending on your status, a bullock, a sheep, a turtle dove or a pigeon would have been offered. God looked upon those offerings equally, taking into consideration each person's resources and means, but the important thing was that the whole of the sacrifice was consumed. In the same way, God wants the sacrifice He receives from our lives to be not just a part (our work or our leisure), but the whole. The apostle Paul put it succinctly in Romans 12:1 when he said,

> *"Therefore, I urge you, brothers, in view of God's mercy, to offer your bodies as living sacrifices, holy and pleasing to God – this is your spiritual act of worship."*

St Benedict started his monastic order with the motto "to work is to pray". Our service is to *be* worship. As somebody once said, "Worship is doing whatever you do to the glory of God."

> *"Whatever you do, whether in word or deed, do all in the name of the Lord Jesus..."*
> (Colossians 3:17)

Influencing others for good

Those who know me well know that I am an avid football fan (or "soccer" as my American friends like to call it). How well I remember times in the playground where I would amaze my friends with my virtuoso skills and repertoire of juggling a tennis ball with my feet. Paddling my feet in tandem with a faded yellow tennis ball I was able to keep the ball off the ground for over a century of mini-kicks. I could even bounce the ball on my head, roll the ball down my back and then, by utilising my state-of-the-art back heel, flip the ball over my right shoulder and on to my right foot. Many hours were spent perfecting this unique skill that I possessed and yet, although I was actually quite a good football player, I never made the grade professionally because I would fail to utilise one particular, very important facet when it came to playing the wider game. That was simply to look up and engage with the other players on the field!

My trials with more accomplished teams convinced me that my tricks and ability to impress through the particular skills I had developed meant nothing unless they were utilised in tandem with the rest of the team. The difference between a professional and an amateur footballer can easily be discerned by the simple fact that the professional will always be looking not primarily at the ball, but at the wider picture of what's

Worship and Mission

happening on the playing field. How he engages with the other players is of the utmost importance.

We can change this world
Through the life we live
It's not the things we say
But the love we give.
If we played our part
What a difference it would make
Soon the world would change
To be a better place.

No one is an island
Our lives are intertwined
Everyone has something they can give
To comfort one another
To lend a helping hand
By showing love and kindness day by day.

Every race and colour
It doesn't matter who you are
We can be a blessing in this world
Each person is important
Special and unique
And we all need to live in harmony.[4]

[4] Dave Bilbrough © 2005 Dave Bilbrough Songs. Taken from the album *This is My Worship*.

Likewise, we can offer individual worship to God, obviously, but it really makes a difference when we look up and engage and participate in the wider arena of what's happening in the world. So often for the worshippers in the Bible, their worship was the birthing place of initiatives and the outworking of a destiny that would have significance, not only for the individuals themselves, but for the many others who by God's grace they would influence and affect.

> "In an age where worship and the pursuit of new, fresh and high quality expressions abound, let's not allow ourselves to get trapped in a kind of Christian parallel universe that sees worship as a kind of fuzzy, warm 'out of body' experience to the detriment of an active participation and partnership with God to make a difference in this world."

This may seem strange coming from a songwriter, but I believe it's not primarily more worship songs that we need right now, rather a greater application of the songs we already sing. We have too narrow a view of what constitutes good worship. My travels to many of the poorer parts of the world and the concerts I have

Worship and Mission

staged there for those outside the church have convinced me that we need to make our worship responses practical as well as spiritual.

In an age where worship and the pursuit of new, fresh and high quality expressions abound, let's not allow ourselves to get trapped in a kind of Christian parallel universe that sees worship as a kind of fuzzy, warm "out of body" experience to the detriment of an active participation and partnership with God to make a difference in this world.

What is worship? – a biblical overview

Worship in the Old Testament went through a process of transformation and development. Numerous events tell the story of how it changed and provide signposts to guide us in our modern-day worship. At times, God revealed His power and presence to individuals – Moses and Abraham were among the many that encountered and experienced His greatness. Exodus 15 tells us of the first hymn to occur in the Bible – a prophetic song sung by Miriam – which stands as an amazing statement about how our worship should be. Starting in verses 1–5 by thanking God for what He'd done, verse 6 gives thanks for who He is and then verses 13–18 move into a prophetic foretelling of what God was going to do.

After this period of appearing primarily to individuals, God then begins to locate Himself in a specific place where His people can come and meet with Him – firstly in the "tent of meeting" and then, once it was built, the temple. Consecrated during the time of Solomon's reign the temple became known as the place where the warrior-king David's plans to instigate 24-hour worship and exuberant praise would be fulfilled. As well as the formal music of the temple, 1 Samuel 10:5–10 tells us how there were spontaneous bands of roaming musicians coming down from the mountains. Added to this, throughout the Bible we see flashes of the prophetic in worship: David would play his music before Saul; the second book of Chronicles tells us how musicians would prophesy with their instruments.

Despite the many references to music and song, the Old Testament draws to a close by underlining the fact that God is not just interested in the sound of our voices or instruments, but primarily in how we practically live out our worship here on earth. Amos 5:23–24 says,

> *"Away with the noise of your songs!*
> *I will not listen to the music of your harps.*
> *But let justice roll on like a river..."*

God was challenging His people on their attitudes towards justice; how they shared their resources and related to those outside the nation of Israel.

Worship and Mission

In the Old Testament a number of distinct aspects set God's people apart in their worship from other religions. One was that they worshipped the One and only God, who was a personal God, not some distant capricious deity; another was that no "images" were permitted to intrude into their relationship with their Creator. It was into this context that Jesus arrived. His encounter with the devil in Matthew 4 shows us how His response was one of submission to God. In His first act of public speaking the Bible tells us that He opened the book and read a familiar passage: *"The Spirit of the Lord is upon me..."* (Luke 4:18 NLT). It was a clear demonstration of how He was to practically live out that worship through social involvement with the world. His obedience, a willing offering to death, revealed His life of service. He fulfilled the Old Testament system of worship by shedding His blood – a direct reference to the Old Testament Passover lamb – and Jesus shows us how, instead of the temple being the place of salvation and blessing, He Himself becomes it. This is central to our core understanding of worship.

Previously, in the Old Testament, entering the "Holy of Holies" without adequate protection was a fatal exercise. Complex rules and laws were put into place to ensure that only a chosen few would experience the tangible presence of God, but at the point of Jesus' death Matthew 27 tells us that the veil representing separation between God and mankind was torn in two.

Sophisticated structures and rituals were no longer the route to God; His presence was now given to all people. The promises of Leviticus 26:12, Jeremiah 31:33, 2 Corinthians 6:16 and Revelation 21:3 that "I will live with them and be their God; they shall be My people" takes us away from a sacred versus secular mentality, where worship took place on special days and special times, into the arena of our worship/our mission being every aspect of our lives. Central to our understanding of worship must be mission.

God calls us to partner with His will and vision. God's vision is that the world will know His Son. Matthew 28:19–20 tells us to "go into all the world". The early disciples had spent time with Jesus becoming familiar with His character and nature. At the culmination of His earthly ministry He commissioned them to take the "Good News" to every culture, land and people.

A royal priesthood

Frequently the Bible refers to the calling of priests to worship. In the Old Testament they were a people set apart; in the New Testament we are all called to be a royal priesthood. Fundamentally, the role of the priest is to minister to God, but also to represent God to others. In the temple of Jerusalem one division of

Worship and Mission

priesthood was called the Levites. Supported financially by the community, they were often musicians whose role was to perform music in extravagant praise to God. The music was majestic and included powerful declarations of God's greatness alongside songs that celebrated festivals, and were sung by massed choirs.

Much of the praise took place in a public manner in areas that were open to the Gentiles as well as the Jews. Israel's worship was not merely to be expressed privately by the people, but in very public ways. People from all cultures travelling the great trade routes from across the eastern world would have passed through the temple courtyards where they would see the colourful, passionate worship of the people of God. Their worship was a testimony to the things that God had done and was doing in their midst. In today's culture a challenge reaches out to us to make God known – the God of our worship – to the wider world.

Today, the role of the prophetic is emphasised a great deal in our worship. Whilst personal prophecy and indeed prophecy directed into a wider arena is important, it is also important to remember that the core meaning of the biblical words used to describe the prophetic means "to speak a divinely inspired message".

Revelation 19:10 (NKJV) tells us that the *"testimony of Jesus is the spirit of prophecy"*. When we are telling of the goodness and kindness of the Lord to a watching world we are truly, I believe, being prophetic; making God and His character known to the broken, the hungry and the needy.

Certainly Paul, in writing to Corinthian church (1 Corinthians 14) raises this when he talks about everyone prophesying and the unbeliever becoming convicted. Prophecy should always result in communication with the world around us.

When Christ is lifted up through our acts of worship and we proclaim His nature and character, then, like iron filings drawn to a magnet, many who do not know Him yet will be drawn to Christ.

Practical expressions

I remember the raised eyebrows on many Christian faces when news filtered through about the praise gatherings going on at a local pub called *The Cauliflower*. Due to a shortage of local halls in the area the upstairs function hall was the only available venue for our regular Sunday night church meetings.

I was part of a small band of Christians newly "baptised in the Spirit", stretching out for more in our expression of church life and wanting to push back the borders of the current worship trends to be a part of something new.

The fervent worship that emerged from that East End

Worship and Mission

location caused quite a stir. On one occasion I recall leaving the meeting while it was in full, joyful flow to visit the Gents' loo downstairs. Looking down over the banister of the big Victorian staircase I spotted the landlord holding the phone receiver up in the air. "That's them up there," he said to his friend, after capturing an audio snapshot of the action, "and it sounds like they're having a much better time up there than we are down here!"

> "What was it Jesus said about the common people hearing Him gladly? Somehow we need to find new ways of taking church to the people, of linking our appreciation of God in worship with practical expressions of mission."

It made me think how infectious and attractive true praise should be to those around us. What was it Jesus said about the common people hearing Him gladly? Somehow we need to find new ways of taking church to the people, of linking our appreciation of God in worship with practical expressions of mission.

My own home church is one where the holistic values of worship and mission are at the core of most if not all of their activities. One example of how we have tried to connect with the world around has been to set up a regular initiative in the region where we meet, in

Worship and Mission

the Spitalfields area of London. It's an area of great cultural diversity – Brick Lane to the right announces a myriad of Curry houses (sampling their delights can be a real treat), and to the left the surrounding areas are known for the club and art scene where a mixture of diverse musical styles attracts an equally diverse group of mainly student-type connoisseurs. This led to our church "taking church" to the people with a regular roster of musicians setting up the p.a., playing music and expressing thankfulness to God in the midst of this environment. It was an opportunity for the church to get out into the marketplace. (I'm personally convinced that the early believers chose to gather in the synagogues not because of the religious connotations, but simply because that was where the people they wanted to reach were located.) The venue we chose was called the *Vibe Bar*, a place where people could easily bring their friends. There would be a positive atmosphere as the musicians would play sometimes structured songs, sometimes improvised, hip-hop, folk, gospel and everything in between, combining worship with mission in a very contemporary sense.

We need to get this good news out to the world! Recently, I have been struck afresh by the fact that as well as there being musicians in the temple (like the musicians in our churches), there were also bands of prophets roaming around being spontaneous, like Ezekiel coming down from the high places to engage with society. What would that look like for musicians in today's arena I wonder? What would it look like for them to carry the Good News?

Global worship

During the mid 1990s, a time where it seemed that a power surge of Holy Spirit activity was taking the world by storm, a friend of mine, Gerald Coates, convened a series of meetings in the heart of London. These ran on a nightly basis for eighteen months at Marsham Street in Westminster. It was a time of commissioning and envisioning alongside receiving the Holy Spirit in fresh ways; God's power was being poured out in this very intense and strategic time. For me personally it proved to be very significant.

Dale Gentry, a visiting prophet from the USA, encouraged us to "enlarge the borders of our tent" and to "walk off of our map"! He stated boldly that "this is the time for breakout to the nations". It certainly made me realise how I had narrowed my own perspectives and expectations in ministry and it rekindled within me a desire to creatively take that spirit of worship to the wider world.

Gradually, I found my worship style beginning to change. It began to represent the down-trodden, the two-thirds world, the oppressed; not necessarily verbalised only through the words, but also in the heartbeat of the music. This resulted in Pat, my wife, who is the percussionist in our band, significantly expanding her collection of instruments to embrace many of the sounds and styles of different nations: Chilean rainsticks augmented orchestral timpani and for one particular large event a huge Chinese gong was hired that filled up most of the rear of the stage! Alongside a new batch of songs that were born at that time I began to pick up something of God's heartbeat for the nations. Feelings of prayer and intercession for the world began to be birthed. This has since led to a number of tours around the world with my band to bless and encourage Christians, but also to work with them in releasing their own musical expressions to God. It has been an exciting experience to see believers expressing their cultural identity in worship: discovering the rhythms of Africa; hearing the sounds of the Western Isles of Scotland. All these, along with sounds from other parts of the world, have helped enrich and diversify my expressions of worship.

> "Authentic worship cannot be put in a bottle and marketed. There is no 'one size fits all'."

On this journey I have learnt so much. Authentic worship cannot be put in a bottle and marketed. There is no "one size fits all". Our worship should be indigenous to the people groups and culture that we are commissioned to reach. This will necessitate both formal and non-formal settings.

African Tardis!

On a recent trip to Kenya with a team of musicians we were invited back to the pastor's house for a traditional Kenyan Sunday lunch. As we sat in a small, cramped, dark room negotiating our way through the local delicacies, the sound of drumming accompanied by occasional singing could be heard from afar.

After finishing our meal we went to investigate. Inside a small ramshackle hut, that didn't look much bigger than a phone booth to me, we found a remarkable sight. It must have been the African Tardis! Squeezed into that tiny space were 50–60 people of all ages playing drums of every description with fantastic control and rhythm – yet at the same time with a completely unselfconscious freedom – a freedom that was, I'm sure, similar to the worship that King David offered who, despite having organised the highly structured processional worship of the temple, also chose to express his freedom in worship by dancing before the Lord in total abandonment.

Indigenous styles

Some musical styles (or particular instruments) in different cultures can be associated with the occult. This does not mean that such instruments or styles cannot be turned around and used for worshipping God, but usually a process of prayerful releasing and redeeming of the style/instrument is necessary.

At a large international conference a few years ago, where many Tamils were present, our friend Jono blew his conch (a large seashell adapted for use as a horn) as an act of worship. This caused considerable dismay among the Tamil Christians who were brought up to believe that the conch could only be blown by someone who was possessed. In their culture they saw it as a demonic manifestation used to summon people to the worship of deviant gods. For us this provided a springboard to discuss and re-examine this important subject. For many people the use of drums and conches could suggest negative and unhelpful influences, however, the Tamils came to realise that the instruments themselves were neutral and could be used to praise the God who redeems all things and delights in our cultural identity. The Tamil believers felt that God was saying it was time to start to use their own cultural instruments again. They had cast them aside, along with all their former beliefs.

Worship and Mission

Having shared some teaching with them they decided to dedicate an actual conch that had come from a Hindu temple in Sri Lanka for the praise of the one true God they had now come to know. Following intensive prayer a dance symbolic of redeeming the conch was performed and it was given to God. A person came and blew it who used to be involved in Hindu temple worship but who had now become a Christian. It was a powerful moment as we witnessed the instrument now being returned to its rightful use.

In Psalm 150 David encourages us to use all the instruments available to us in our praise. The bagpipes of Scotland, Asian tablas and the balalaikas of Russia can all be used in our worship just as much as the keyboard, guitar or synthesiser. Just because some of these sounds are unfamiliar to the Western ear does not mean that they are not heard and cherished by our Father in Heaven. We need to stress that through Christ's death and resurrection all believers, regardless of colour and culture, are new creations in Him. We must not fall into the trap of thinking that our cultural preferences in worship are the correct way to "do" worship to the exclusion of others. God looks for authentic and diverse expressions of worship from all the people groups of the globe.

EQ – heart of worship and a call to the world

Recently, Pat and I have been heading up a regular gathering for musicians involved in a variety of spheres and callings – from those in the worship ministry to those in the mainstream music industry. EQ, as it is called, exists to promote fellowship, encouragement and dialogue, and provides a safe place where established and emerging musicians, DJs, songwriters, producers, teachers, worship leaders and performers can gather together with the aim of promoting a heart for worship and recognising our call out to the world.

There are many excellent conferences and seminars for church worship groups and all of these have their place, but I feel that it is very important that our worship embraces a true vision of worship that involves mission. Prayer and encouragement are a regular feature of our times together, but often that encouragement takes the form of expanding our pre-suppositions as to what it means to be a worshipper. As I see it many musicians who are in the mainstream arena need to have a real appreciation of the value and importance of worship, but, conversely, many of our worship teams need to think beyond the four walls of their sanctuary and discover the joys and challenges of taking that worship to the world.

Worship and Mission

Jermyn Street

For me this has resulted in a desire to reach out in mission in a slightly unorthodox way by arranging a series of concerts aimed at the non-churched in a theatre in the West End of London called Jermyn Street.

I spotted the theatre on my frequent journeys across town and always felt there was something unique about it. Increasingly, as I became convinced of the need to "cross over" taking my worship and witness into the wider world, it settled within me that this was a great place to start. Often when passing by I would stand outside for a short while and offer up some heartfelt prayers. "Open the doors," I would say to God. Then, one day, as I was standing outside, the doors literally opened and upon seeing me a member of the theatre staff asked if he could be of help. I walked down the steps and saw inside the small, intimate venue that was to be the perfect launch pad for this initiative to reach the wider world. I started to talk to the management about the possibility of booking the theatre and putting on an event there.

Over a period of time I began the process of hosting a number of musical concerts with my band, where I would not only share some of my self-written Christian material, but also mix in songs that have influenced me down through the years, telling my story, my life journey of growing up in the East End of London and

Worship and Mission

becoming aware of the power of music and the power of faith. Songs ranging from Paul Simon classics, Fats Waller and Nora Jones were included as reference points to those in the audience who had no church background. Underpinning everything we have done in these events has been the message that God is good; He is kind and can be trusted. It's an evening of "worship", but in an unconventional way – camouflaged at times in order to entice the non-believer towards the Good News.

"Prophecy" is for the edification of the Church, but it's also to speak out to the world. If we as worshippers are supposed to be prophetic, then we must connect with the world outside our churches. The feedback from the Jermyn Street experience has been positive as people have brought friends from outside the church to be exposed to the truth of the Gospel that many are hearing for the first time.

Obviously, we still need worship in the church – but that spirit of praise should journey beyond the church walls. In this day we need to see worship rising in different ways. Every congregation, every church, has its own voice and a unique expression of the diversity of gifts that God gives. Each gathering of believers, therefore, will find their own natural ways of connecting and being aware of what's going on in the world outside. We need not only to display the divinity of Jesus, but also to display our humanity to the world and not be afraid to exhibit it and simply be who we are. Our

Worship and Mission

musicians shouldn't get locked into playing worship choruses to the exclusion of other forms of music. Many would benefit from learning to take that worshipping heart out to the people of the world with other musical expressions and lead them into an encounter with God.

> This is our commission
> To fill the air with praise
> And to tell the people of this world
> The glory of His name
> With thousands upon thousands
> From every tribe and tongue
> We cry worthy is the Lamb once slain
> For He has overcome
>
> *Show your glory, show your glory*
> *Show your glory over all the earth*[5]

Play skilfully

Music can also be a powerful force for mission by providing opportunities in the most unexpected situations...

[5] Dave Bilbrough, "The Voice of God is Calling" © 2000 Thankyou Music, taken from the album *Personal Worship*.

> Worship and Mission

In Victorian times, when William Booth was active in his ministry, to play in a brass band was something that many people of his era aspired to. By forming the Salvation Army band Booth was providing an opportunity for people to play on their instruments in praise to God, but he was also providing an important doorway through which they could be drawn in and involved in the life of the church. Church statistician, Peter Brierley, once said that, "many people come to an experience of faith in our disconnected society by feeling a sense of belonging prior to believing".

> **"The music we use in worship can provide a way for many people to engage with and encounter God for the first time."**

Similarly, the music we use in worship can provide a way for many people to engage with and encounter God for the first time. Popular worship leader Kate Simmonds came to faith by joining a gospel choir at Kensington Temple in London. Her enthusiasm for singing drew her to gospel music and her involvement in the choir began a journey that eventually led to her finding the source of that music – Christ.

Simon, the guitarist in my band, asked a Christian producer friend of mine, Andy Piercy, to work with him and his brother on their mainstream secular album. Out

Worship and Mission

of that relationship Andy asked Simon, at the time a non-Christian, to come on various occasions and play in the worship band at his church, Holy Trinity Brompton in London. Simon took the opportunity and experienced not only a great level of musicianship, but something of the presence of Christ in the worship. Eventually Andy was able to invite Simon to an Alpha course which led to him giving his life to Christ.

Once when I was telling Simon's story at a worship conference in Hungary, the local church leader was so inspired (and so thin on the ground with local musicians) that he visited his local jazz club and invited some of the best players to play in the worship team at his church! This ultimately led them to commit their lives to Christ. Here is a splendid example of worship being an access point for people who do not know Christ.

Paul, writing to the Philippians, talks about us holding out the word of life; Paul tells us to declare His wonderful deeds. The praise and the worship of God which should be our most creative and inspiring expression provides us with tremendous evangelistic opportunities when combined with the integrity of a worshipping heart. Paul and Silas in the Philippian jail, around about midnight, were declaring their praise to God when a miracle occurred which resulted in the jailer coming under conviction himself and experiencing new birth. We should not be surprised when hearts and lives are changed through the power of worship.

Worship and Mission

Sing joyfully

Pat, my wife, is an experienced and accomplished choral director. People recognise in her the heart of a worshipper and as a result she has frequently been asked to lead large gatherings of Christians in vocal praise to God. Alongside this her work as a schoolteacher has created opportunities for her children's choir to be involved with various worship projects including the Spring Harvest *Kid's Praise* albums. Since many of these children come from non-Christian backgrounds it is wonderful to see them given the opportunity to actively engage with the Gospel as they sing. Many come from other faiths and yet they still take the songs away with them to practise, filling their homes with the truths of the Gospel!

A year or two back Pat received an unexpected phone call from a BBC producer. She began the conversation by saying, "I expect you want to speak to Dave?" but the producer replied, "No, it's you I want. I would like your choir to sing on a programme that will be televised at the end of the year as part of the end of the year celebrations." Pat tried to find out what the programme was about but the producer said she was not allowed to say.

A sense of mystery enshrouded the project, which prohibited the producer from revealing what this particular programme was about. So it was with some

Worship and Mission

caution that Pat, having obtained permission from the school headmaster for a camera crew to come into the school, arranged for her choir to be filmed singing one piece. In fact, the degree of secrecy caused quite a lot of discussion and no small degree of anxiety. What would the footage be used for? Could it be a satirical item designed to give her school and schools like it a bad name?

One morning, whilst reflecting on this, I suddenly remembered an unusual occurrence that happened in Toronto some years back where, at the height of the "Toronto Blessing" at the Airport Christian Fellowship, Pat and I were asked to lead worship. After the meeting had finished, Patricia Bootsma, one of the leaders at the time, requested to pray over Pat and myself. For me she prayed blessing; for Pat she prophesied that God was giving singing back to her in a new way, and that she could see Pat one day singing over the Royal Family. I must admit that my reaction was to give that particular prophetic word a wide berth. "I can never see that happening," I thought to myself, "that's one for the back burner. She must have got a little bit over-excited about the fact that we're British!" Nevertheless, that particular morning the recollection of this event popped into my head and suddenly it all made sense. "It's for the Queen's speech," I said excitedly to Pat. "Your choir will be singing on the Queen's speech, don't you remember the prophecy?" Sure enough, a few days later, confirmation was given by the producer who had been told by her seniors not to reveal this information too early.

How amazing that a prophecy which seemed so incredible a few years back was being fulfilled before our eyes. To sing songs of worship before the head of the British Commonwealth and a worldwide audience was a fantastic honour. We took it as confirmation that Pat's work with these children was part of God's intended plan for her and the choir. Here was worship and mission active in a very grass roots way. It was wonderful that they were singing a song of praise to God and provided such a brilliant picture of how cultures working together can promote harmony.

God's praise cannot and should not be entrapped within four walls alone!

God's heart is for the whole world

(Read Isaiah 61:11; 66:18–19)

In 1793 William Carey set sail for India. Years later C.T. Studd embarked on a ministry that would develop into a lifelong identification with people of the Belgian Congo in Africa. Many of these early missionaries took their coffins with them on their journeys, fully expecting they would not return back to their home shores alive! I marvel at the stories of the missionary endeavours of men and women who fearlessly went into un-reached and unknown lands for the Gospel, leaving loved ones behind at great personal sacrifice. Much of their legacy has been amazingly positive and tremendously fruitful, however, some of the negative aspects have been the "colonialisation" of the Gospel and the mass export of *Hymns Ancient and Modern* – in other words, imposing Western ideas about how to "do" church and Western styles that dictated how musical expressions of worship should be executed.

> **"Let's not allow ourselves to become stereotypical in our thinking, encamping around a 'contemporary worship' banner that owes much of its existence to the 1980s rather than the current musical climate. Each generation has a new song to sing and it will be different from the style of the last generation."**

Contrary to popular belief, music is not a universal language. There are many languages in music just as there are many languages that are spoken. A musical expression that touches the heart of someone in Prague is quite different from that which moves someone in Mumbai, India. Across the musical genres, and indeed age groups, there are many subtleties and nuances of great variety that stir the soul. We are allowed preferences, but not prejudices when it comes to worship. Increasingly, the role of the ethnomusicologist has become a valuable one working with remote tribes, learning the musical vocabulary of people groups and encouraging indigenous expression.

God wants us to be authentic. We must be real about who we are. God wants to connect with our culture to meet us where we are. In cities across the world many of the youth have embraced the MTV culture so that they now value Western musical expressions. Here I think we need to learn to fuse together different styles to create something of the "new song" that the Bible often talks about. We have an opportunity to fuse and remix musical styles that affirm cultural values and flavours, whilst recognising the current trends of various people groups.

This is something of the spiritual legacy handed down to us as Christians. It was the reformist Martin Luther who took the music of songs from the taverns and introduced words of praise in a way that was radical and groundbreaking in the Christian landscape of his time. Wesley did the same.

Today, in the West, we live in a culture of rap, hip-hop, R & B, soul and a bewildering array of other musical styles. Let's not allow ourselves to become stereotypical in our thinking, encamping around a "contemporary worship" banner that owes much of its existence to the 1980s rather than the current musical climate. Each generation has a new song to sing and it will be different from the style of the last generation.

Worship and Mission

Over the years I've had the privilege of attending a multitude of diverse Christian gatherings of every style imaginable: sitting in rows, sitting in a circle, half-circle, sitting on the floor, sitting in pews (ouch!), sitting on chairs; being 45 minutes in from the official start-time with people still chatting and realising that the meeting had actually begun at the arranged time; singing in mud huts in the jungle, glorious English cathedrals, theatres, cinemas, stadiums; to young people, old people and everything in between; I've even sung in an abattoir and a boxing ring!

Despite having ample opportunity to say what a Christian gathering should look like, the New Testament writers had very little to say about the style of our worship meetings. They were only interested in the content. Style is irrelevant except that it should reflect our culture and background. Jesus Christ wants Himself to be uniquely expressed through each church situation. The Old Covenant prescribes set forms of worship that will point us to the new, but now the external rituals have been replaced by an internal spiritual reality. This leaves us free to jettison prescriptive, patterned procedures and to explore the spontaneous, unique and indigenous expressions arising from our gifts, our skills and our geographic location. If our worship is to engage in mission we need to connect with the styles and culture that are surrounding us and avoid the temptation to isolate ourselves from fashions in music and social trends.

Worship and Mission

Whether we are traditional, emergent or liquid, it's OK. What brings it all together is our new birth in Christ, for in and through Christ all things are brought into unity. The New Testament concludes that there will be a new heaven and a new earth where God is praised in every language (Revelation 7:9; 14:6); it teaches that people of all cultures will walk in God's light (Revelation 21:4); that all nations will be healed (Revelation 22:2). Our distinctive cultural flavour is made all the richer as we play our part in tandem with others, but joined together by the head, who is Christ.

Multi-coloured praise

In the early days of my development as a worship leader our small church began a journey away from our traditional Baptist roots with its hymn-prayer sandwich, towards the exploration of a more charismatic style of worship. We teamed up for a regular joint meeting with our "brothers and sisters" from across the town, whose heritage was from the local Pentecostal church. With flutes, guitars, and armed with plenty of tambourines, our motley worship group undertook a crash course in experiencing different church cultures. As the main worship leader from our Baptist group, I was to encounter Colin – at 6′ 3″ with strapping muscles, blond hair and a beard, an imposing

| Worship and Mission |

character – and our gathered worship became a somewhat interesting collision of church styles arising from our different backgrounds. I would lead off, usually with a reverent, meaningful, mid-tempo expression of musical worship. My Baptist friends would rise to their feet in solemn and dignified response. However, two or three songs down the line and at the cue of the Pentecostal section of the congregation, Colin would strike out with a medley of up-beat, toe-tapping rousers designed to shake off our self-created worship blues, or at least that's how he perceived it! Colin's gang would enthusiastically rise and embrace this change of musical direction. We (Baptists), however, would slump back into our chairs, pushing our corporate "miss" buttons and waiting for a sufficient gap in the music during which our own team of musicians would lead us "back" into the "true" presence of God!

It became a kind of spiritual table-tennis. A to-ing and fro-ing based on our musical preferences, our backgrounds and, dare I say it, our traditions. Eventually I realised, not only did we need direction set from one main leader, but we also needed to embrace some of Colin's youthful exuberance. Colin, as he humbly acknowledged, also needed to gain a deeper appreciation of our more reflective worship style.

As a resident of Greater London, on any given day I am able to witness the rich cultural diversity that is constantly being displayed. During a stroll down

Tottenham Court Road, Brazilians, Jamaicans, Indians, Vietnamese and Eastern Europeans can all be observed. I am reliably informed that there are now more black churches in our capital than white. Brazilians are sending Christian missionaries to re-evangelize our country. Increasingly, we are living in a multi-racial society. I am committed to a worship that makes room for this reality and actively learns from different ways and styles that are accepted models of "radical worship". God is bigger, broader and more colourful than any of our worship preferences.

In an age where isolation and alienation abound in our society; where so many feel disconnected one from another; where, in the UK, the divorce rate is the third highest in the world and 40% of children are born out of wedlock, many are looking and longing simply "to belong". Therefore, part of our mission must include holistic worship that expresses and reflects a cross-generational bond, uniting us in Christ.

Worship is an event and a lifestyle

Worship is undoubtedly the lifestyle of an individual heart offered up to God. However, there are unquestionably times where we are called to gather together to set ourselves apart as God's community, distinct from, but co-existing with the world. In Old

Worship and Mission

Testament times the festivals that were regularly celebrated were strategic gatherings where all the tribes, each with their own distinct character, would join together as one. Recently I have been privileged to have been involved with a number of significant events where the Church has gathered on a wide-scale basis, overriding generational or denominational preferences, with one golden aim – to see Jesus glorified.

In the mid-eighties it was Graham Kendrick who, building on the precedent set by the pioneering Salvation Army many years before, called the church together for a Carnival of Praise, which was later to be known as the "Make-Way Marches". Multitudes around the globe joined together to worship with songs, banners and peaceful marching so that their worship would be a witness to the watching world, both in cities and villages. Many stories have been told of how God touched, spoke to and blessed bystanders through these acts of worship.

In the mid-nineties it was Noel Richards who had a vision for gathering Christians together in stadiums around the world. This vision found fruition in 1997 where at Wembley Stadium, England's premier football arena and scene of the 1966 World Cup (which incidentally England won!) 45,000 people gathered for a "worship concert". It was a powerful and moving sight to see in the midst of the worship many people give their lives to God for the first time at this very public event.

In 2006 the Olympic Stadium in Berlin was another part of Noel's vision for Christians around Europe to unite together and allow their worship to become a witness to the watching world. We need events like this that are the expression of a worshipping lifestyle.

Evangelistic worship

Popular American singer-songwriter, Don Francisco, has had a significant impact over the years in the United Kingdom. I remember being asked to tour with him – Don as a performer with his story-type songs; me as a worship leader armed with songs to lead people in God's praise. In addition there was an evangelist to conclude each evening with an invitation for people to come to know Christ. These large-scale events took place all across the country, but somehow did not quite seem to click into gear. Although no reflection on each individual's contribution, the expected evangelistic harvest was not as evident as we had hoped for. The format of the evening was simple: I led some worship, Don sang and the evangelist tied it all together with an appeal. But one night everything changed. I had already sung and was backstage expecting Don to perform; yet as he stood on stage he chose to forsake his prearranged set list and instead launched into yet more worship. The worship continued and I must

Worship and Mission

confess I scratched my head a little, asking myself why Don should be leading the worship – surely that was my job? Right in the midst of this environment of worship he made an altar call for people to come forward and commit their lives to God. "Surely that is the job of the evangelist," I thought, "no one will respond!" Yet, to my amazement, that night hundreds streamed forward. A breakthrough had occurred. Our mission had been executed in the midst of our worship.

Worship and mission are inextricably linked. We should therefore look for opportunities to make the truth of the Gospel accessible to people as God is being lifted up in our midst. What was that that Jesus said again? *"I, when I am lifted up ... will draw all men to myself"* (John 12:32).

Another time I was on tour in the North of England. The evening was going well. There had been a great release of praise. I had shared a few new songs as well as some familiar ones. In this environment of worship I was struck by a feeling that wouldn't go away. As I looked out at the congregation, four rows back to my left I saw a young woman. Straight into my heart came some words and I spoke them out directly to her: "God has heard your prayer and is pleased that you are opening up to Him. He wants to reveal His love in a personal way to you tonight – to bring you to a place where you have not been before and lead you into His peace." The music moved on, we sang and the meeting

Worship and Mission

finished. As we went through our nightly ritual of clearing the stage she excitedly came up to me.

"How did you know?" she said.

"How did I know what?" I replied.

"Tonight, as you said what you did to me, I was asking God to come into my life. I want to become a Christian."

We should expect God to speak to us as we worship.

Bringing healing

I'd just put down the phone and I must admit I was really quite chuffed to have been invited to lead worship at a prestigious leaders' gathering, which I knew would give me an opportunity to join with many seasoned national ministries in worship. This was going to be great! However, as any worship leader would understand, those feelings of quiet satisfaction quickly evaporated, turning into feelings of sheer panic as I weighed up in my mind which worship songs would be the right ones for the occasion. In the days leading up to the event every stroll down the street was accompanied with my own dialogue with God as I pondered this important question. As I was turning the corner of a street, not too far away from my house, out of the blue God seemed to speak into my spirit. It is a voice that I can't always explain, that is rarely audible,

Worship and Mission

but I just know it's Him. "Sing 'Holy Fire from Heaven'," He seemed to be saying.

I quickly stored this information in my heart and later pulled down the words from the internet as I was not completely familiar with it. I began practising and memorising the words and the chords. As my choice of songs for the day emerged, "Holy Fire" was well and truly in the set list. Eventually, the day itself came. The guitar was taken out of its case and wholeheartedly I entered in and led others in the worship, eagerly awaiting the execution of the song that I felt God had particularly steered me towards, believing that in this company of mature experienced believers surely revival would break out! The moment came – the song was released to the congregation. To my amazement and disappointment, nothing obvious happened! Although politely received the song did not result in the expected breakthrough I was believing for. I sang it round again; certain I couldn't have got it wrong, but shortly afterwards abandoned it for a more familiar anthem. The meeting ended and, rather crestfallen, I hastily boxed up my guitar and headed for the door.

"What a disappointment," I thought to myself. "Well, I must have got that wrong." Just as I was about to turn into the corridor that led to the glass exit doors and the safety of my chalet, a middle-aged lady tapped me on the shoulder.

"I need to speak to you," she said. "During the worship time I was physically healed. My shoulders and my arms were somehow released to move freely again in a way that they haven't done for years."

"Oh," I said, rather shocked. These words of encouragement really were living water to my soul. "When did it happen?" I asked.

"Instantly," she replied, "the moment you started up that song."

"Which song?" I asked, as there had been several.

"Holy Fire from Heaven," she replied.

It was a valuable lesson for me to learn. To understand that we can't always discern the movings of God with our natural eye, but also that yet again, in an environment of worship, God wanted to fulfil His mission to set yet another prisoner free. As we worship we must expect changes, revelation and healing, expressions of mission to be released.

Implications of His grace

It was on a youth weekend that I first heard the claims of Jesus clearly presented to me. I found it very thought provoking and began a quest for truth that lasted for some months. I didn't want to be carried along by the crowd. I wanted an experience that was real. "God, if You are there, give me faith to believe in You," was my constant prayer. One September night, confounded by the glorious simplicity of it all, I knelt

Worship and Mission

by my bed and asked Jesus to come into my life. A sense of gratitude filled me as Jesus revealed His love and acceptance for someone as insignificant as me. I was overwhelmed with joy.

> It's time to make a declaration
> that I will live my life for you.
> The fields are white for harvest
> the labourers are few.
> Yes, whatever Lord, you ask me
> I will do.
>
> This is my worship
> This is my worship
> This is my worship to you
> (repeat)[6]

These last few years more implications of His grace have come into focus for me as I've seen how His heart has a special place for the oppressed and the overlooked in this world. The Jesus I worship calls me to care for the poor and to lift up the needs of those less fortunate than myself. The common people heard Him gladly while the Pharisees tried to trip Him up with their smug self-righteousness. Our prestige and illusions of power have never been important to Him.

[6] *It's Time to Make a Declaration*, Dave Bilbrough © 2005 Dave Bilbrough Songs.

Surely the experience of being touched by His grace-filled heart can only increase our compassion for the vast majority of the world who live daily in poverty and deprivation.

Protest march and revival meeting

Jesus came to seek and save that which was lost (Luke 19:10). God wants to draw many to His Kingdom to find new life and forgiveness of sins through Jesus. Unquestionably, He calls us to go out into all the world to preach the Gospel, but sometimes I feel we have narrowed our understanding of what our mission is and, indeed, what that Gospel message really is. The manifesto that Jesus publicly announced was that He had come to heal the broken-hearted, to bring good news to the poor, to give sight to the blind. It was an holistic message awakening us yet again to see the heart of God and how it beats for all people. There are 2,000 scriptural references to God's compassion for the poor. The Bible says that God is a lover of righteousness and cares for the poor and marginalised. Micah – a village peasant turned prophet – raised issues with the powers of Jerusalem that would challenge their prosperity, security and the preservation of the status quo. He provides just one example among many. God always has been and is committed to the plight of the poor.

Worship and Mission

Issues of aid, trade and debt are ones that we as Christians should not be afraid to address. They are part of our mission, other facets of our expression of worship. This statistic makes interesting reading: it takes 9 working minutes to earn enough to purchase a McDonald's Big Mac in Chicago. In Los Angeles and Miami it takes 10 minutes; in New York 12 minutes; and in Nairobi, Kenya, approximately 181 minutes. Whilst McDonalds may not be my favourite food and certainly is not a necessity, it is an amazing example of the imbalanced nature of the global economic system. As Bono said in his significant address given at a presidential prayer breakfast, "The only time Jesus is judgmental is on the subject of the poor. 'As you have done to the least of these, my brethren, you have done it unto me' (Matthew 25:40)." Each day 650 Africans die as a result of preventable, treatable diseases. In our Western world we live in an era where rich people are thin and poor people are fat. It used to be the other way around in Charles Dickens' time.

Alongside the opportunities we provide for church members to respond to altar calls and receive personal ministry, we should also be encouraging our congregations to turn the focus away from themselves and to look outwards. We need to show people that they can actively write to legislators concerning appropriate issues and see this as a valid act of worship. We need revival meetings *and* protest marches!

In 1906 the Azuza Street outpouring in California heralded the beginning for many of the modern-day Charismatic movement. Frank Bartleman, an early participant, noted, "the colour line was washed away by the blood". At a time where the Ku Klux Klan symbolised the prejudices and hatred that reigned in the attitudes between whites and blacks, the interracial aspects of this revival movement provided a striking contrast of the racism and segregation of the time. Black and white stood together in this abandoned warehouse on Azuza Street. Surely here's an example to us all. Where ethnic cleansing and racial bigotry are still very present in our world, the Gospel and its impact must surely reawaken us to the equality of all people.

Ecology – environment

This world in which we live does not belong to us. As the Scripture proclaims loudly, *"The earth is the LORD's, and everything in it"* (Psalm 24:1).

Together we share our lives here on an earth full of such beauty and diversity. Flowers, grass and trees enhance our environment. A multitude of fish, birds, insects and animals inhabit our world and live alongside us. *"Everything was created through him"* says John 1:3 (The Message). There is a diversity of life

Worship and Mission

on this planet ranging from the oceans to the lands, the people to the wildlife. Isaiah 6:3 (NKJV) declares, *"The whole earth is full of His glory"* and Colossians 1:17 says, *"... in* [Christ] *all things hold together"*. The imprint of His Spirit pervades the whole universe in which we live.

An old Celtic traditional prayer says these words:

> "There is no plant in the ground but tells of your beauty, O Christ, there is no creature on earth, there is no life in the sea but proclaims your goodness. There is no bird on the wing, there is no star in the sky, there is nothing beneath the sun but is full of your blessing. Lighten our understanding of your presence all around, O Christ, and kindle our will to be caring for the creation."

Our mission includes the care for our natural world.

Genesis 1:1-2 tells us of how God created this world and brought order that we might manage and tend His creation. Mankind was given responsibility to nurture and love creation, to be stewards of the earth, but sadly, as we have come out of alignment with God's intended plan, it has led to covetousness and greed towards our natural resources. Many of the good gifts that God has given have been used and abused, often to the detriment of the vulnerable and the poor. The challenge for us in our mission is to be a prophetic witness, upholding Kingdom values as we cherish and conserve the earth that God has given. Philippians 2:3 (NKJV) says, *"Let nothing be done through selfish ambition or conceit."* We need to ensure we demonstrate a generosity of spirit and a sharing of the earth's natural resources for all mankind.

The people of the Bible lived with the consciousness of God being very present in our natural, created world. In their writings they reflected this. The Psalms are full of appreciation for God's wonderful creation. Hills and valleys speak to us of His saving power; human frailty is represented through imagery of grass and flowers that will one day wither away; God's tender love is portrayed by the gentle shepherding skills of the shepherd. Psalm 65 speaks of not only His history of redemption, but reminds us that our Creator is the giver of all good gifts to this earth. Paul in Romans 8:18–25 tells us how all creation is in labour to see the coming King.

God did not confine Himself to meeting with mankind only in the temple. Many divine appointments took place in the deserts and the mountains, the hillsides and valleys, in the middle of the sea and even in the deepest pit or in the confines of a prison cell. God wants to reveal Himself everywhere.

I remember the time I spent with my team taking a series of workshops and seminars on worship in the wondrous western part of Scotland called the Isle of

Skye. During the course of one of the seminars, as I was speaking about how we need to celebrate the God of creation, it seemed so fitting to lead this motley group of musicians, with violins, drums and guitars, outside the tent to express their praise to God; to be thankful for the beauty surrounding; to sing to the hills and the trees of the goodness and kindness of God, rather than be sheltered and surrounded in the safe confines of the meeting tent. God is all around to be worshipped and celebrated. Our worship was made all the richer by participating with all creation; where "the trees of the fields shall clap their hands" and to quote Jesus "even the rocks will cry out" in acknowledgement of His mighty power and saving grace.

The Gospel is a call to people everywhere to worship

"Let the peoples praise You, O God."
(Psalm 67:3 NKJV)

"Declare his glory among the nations."
(Psalm 96:3)

Paul's heart for mission was insatiable. Tirelessly he endured beatings, prison and shipwrecks for the sake of the Gospel. Down through the centuries his passion for reaching others with the Good News is unsurpassed. Romans 15:16 clearly shows that he saw his role and ministry fundamentally as a priest to God – viewing the Gentile souls that he had led to Christ as his offerings of worship. Evangelism was an integral part of his worship, not merely a personal response, but a response on behalf of others. From a place of persecuting Christians he gladly and freely gave himself, seeing his passion for the lost as an act of worship, inviting everyone to participate in the worship of the One who had saved him and could do the same for others. To quote popular writer and theologian John Piper, "Out of praise comes mission, and out of mission comes praise."

God's aim is to make people everywhere a people of praise (Psalm 67:3–4). His declared intention is that everyone might be a worshipper. True meaning is found in life as we look not into ourselves, as the New Age gurus would have us believe, but with gratitude and gratefulness towards our Creator and Redeemer. We are called to share with others the kindness and goodness of God because we have experienced it ourselves.

There are many things I do not understand about the book of Revelation. I am challenged by the images it presents, many of which don't fit comfortably into my mindset or current experience, however, fundamentally I know it's a book about worship. Revelation chapters 5–7 describe for us the magnificence as God's people

Worship and Mission

from every tribe and every language harmonise together – a glorious mosaic of praising people fixed with their eyes upon the Lamb who is right at the centre, the One who has overcome. In eternity barriers of inequality and injustice are broken down. Suffering and homelessness are no more as Christ the Lamb is seen majestic in His reign upon the throne. There will be no need for mission for all things will have reached completion. However, until that day when we see Him face to face we are to be a "Kingdom of Priests" here on earth, called to herald and create a glorious crescendo of global worship – a worship that finds expression in mission here on earth as we affirm the King and His Kingdom to all people and present the life-changing, soul-saving, world-redeeming message of the Gospel.

> We won't back down or stand in silence
> While famine, Aids and debt divide us
> We'll live to bring God's kingdom to this earth.
> The chains that bind of greed and anger
> Jealous pride and exploitation
> Can be broken by His saving love.
> There's so much pain and confusion
> In this world that we live
> But to each of us His Spirit has been given
> To bring good news, to bring good news.

Worship and Mission

Our voice will sound for truth and justice
For victims of discrimination
The homeless and forgotten of this world.
We won't back down, we're moving forward
Bringing hope to those where fallen
Lifting high the message of the cross.
We long to see transformation
We pray for peace on this earth
And to each of us His Spirit has been given
To bring good news, to bring good news.

His light will shine in every nation
When we turn our words to action
Then the world will see that Christ is Lord
For we are called to feed the hungry
Reach the poor with love and mercy
'Cause everybody's special in His eyes.
God's heart is filled with compassion
For every person in need
And to each of us His Spirit has been given
To bring good news, to bring good news.[7]

---

[7] Dave Bilbrough, © 2005 Dave Bilbrough Songs. Taken from the album *This is My Worship*.

Dave Bilbrough
This is my worship
New DVD and CD out now!
All new, original songs, filmed as a live concert in an intimate unplugged setting in the historic Spitalfields area of London.
All profits towards developing worship initiatives in parts of the world which cannot afford to host worship events, commonplace in the affluent West.
Dave Bilbrough
This is my worship
Dave Bilbrough
This is my worship
www.davebilbrough.com

About the author

With a wide appeal that spans all Christian denominations, Dave Bilbrough's songs have become a staple part of many church repertoires. Recent years have seen Dave developing a vision towards integrating musical influences from around the world to create authentic new sounds of worship. Alongside his music he is in regular demand as a seminar speaker on themes related to worship. His ministry brings an emphasis on the grace and faithfulness of God, and uninhibited praise and reconciliation. Dave is a patron of Mildmay Mission Hospital.

For further information on Dave's ministry, including tour dates and albums visit the Dave Bilbrough website www.davebilbrough.com

In addition to regular travelling and touring as a worship leader/speaker in the UK and the US, Dave frequently travels to many of the poorer parts of the world that cannot afford to host worship and training events. His latest album, *This is My Worship* was produced to help raise funds for further initiatives in these regions. If you would like to partner with Dave and Pat in financial or prayerful support of these missions please contact them via email:

> strum@davebilbrough.com

or write to them at:

> Dave Bilbrough
> PO Box 2612
> Romford
> Essex RM2 5YB

We hope you enjoyed reading this New Wine book.
For details of other New Wine books
and a range of 2,000 titles from other
Word and Spirit publishers visit our website:
www.newwineministries.co.uk